Fired Up

How Emotional Intelligence Fuels Effective Communication

Table of Contents

Chapter 1. Introduction

Welcome to our Special Report, 'Fired Up: How Emotional Intelligence Fuels Effective Communication'! This captivating report heralds a bright new perspective on harnessing your feelings for successful communication. Grounded in the latest research but presented in an appealing, easy-to-follow manner, this report articulates the pivotal role that emotional intelligence can play in boosting our communication skills. Imagining a world where every conversation fuels connection and understanding, rather than confusion or conflict? This report brings us inches closer to realizing that dream. Buckle up for a delightful exploration of how tapping into our emotional reservoir can turn us into effective communicators. Don't wait around - the keys to revolutionizing your conversations lie within the pages of our report. Ready to transform your discourse? Invest in our Special Report now and tune into the power of emotional intelligence!

Chapter 2. Laying the Foundations: Emotional Intelligence Explained

Emotional Intelligence (EI), typically defined as the ability to recognize, understand, and manage our emotions, as well as that of others, has been intensely studied and proven to be a critical factor in social interaction and communication. People with high emotional intelligence have a keen awareness of their emotional state and can use this understanding to steer their behavior, navigate social complexities, and make personal decisions that yield positive results.

2.1. What is Emotional Intelligence?

Understanding the concept of emotional intelligence is pivotal to harnessing its power. Emotional intelligence comprises a broad range of skills, typically divided into four main domains by psychologist and bestselling author Daniel Goleman. These domains include:

1. Self-awareness: This involves the ability to recognize and understand personal moods and motivations, and their effects on others.

2. Self-management: This includes the ability to control or redirect disruptive impulses and moods, and the propensity to suspend judgment to think before acting.

3. Social awareness: This pertains to the ability to understand the emotional makeup of other people and the skill to treat people according to their emotional reactions.

4. Relationship management: This encompasses the proficiency in managing relationships, building networks, and the ability to find

common ground and build rapport.

The first step toward understanding and improving emotional intelligence is to gain a working knowledge of these four domains, and how they work in concert to determine our interactions with others.

2.2. The Role of Emotional Intelligence in Personal and Professional Life

Emotionally intelligent people fare better on multiple fronts - be it personal relationships, health, or professional life.

In personal relationships, individuals who are emotionally smart maintain better relationships. They can predict and understand their feelings and those of others, leading to balanced and fulfilling interpersonal relationships.

In the context of health, individuals with high emotional intelligence are better equipped to understand and manage stress, contributing to better physical and mental health.

In professional life, those high in emotional intelligence tend to be better leaders. They understand their team members' emotional state and adapt their communication and management style accordingly, leading to improved team dynamism and productivity.

Emotional intelligence profoundly impacts our day-to-day life, and better understanding this concept enables us to harness its power and influence our overall success positively.

2.3. Emotional Intelligence and Communication

When it comes to communication, emotional intelligence plays a significant role, because effective communication extends beyond words. Emotionally intelligent people can detect and interpret emotions in verbal, non-verbal, and written communication methods, picking up subtle cues that others might miss. This ability enriches their communication and makes them effective communicators. Moreover, high emotional intelligence equips individuals to respond to communications more effectively, because they can understand and control their emotions, helping to maintain clear and open communication.

2.4. Components of Emotional Intelligence

Let's dive deeper into the components of emotional intelligence. An understanding of the five key parameters - Self-awareness, Self-regulation, Motivation, Empathy, and Social Skills, known as the 'Goleman model, will help us comprehend emotional intelligence in far greater depth.

1. Self-Awareness: Emotionally intelligent individuals are aware of their emotions and how they affect their actions. They recognize their weaknesses and strengths, have a strong sense of self-worth, and exude confidence.

2. Self-Regulation: These individuals don't impulsively react; instead, these are people who can manage their emotions and impulses, following up on commitments, and adapt to changing circumstances.

3. Motivation: Emotionally intelligent people are motivated individuals. They're productive, love a challenge, and are highly

effective in whatever they do.

4. Empathy: These individuals can identify with and understand the wants, needs, and viewpoints of those around them.

5. Social Skills: Individuals with excellent social skills are good at managing disputes, are excellent communicators, and understand how to build and maintain relationships.

Each of these components is interrelated and combines to define our emotional intelligence. By understanding each component and working on self-improvement in these areas, one can enhance their emotional intelligence, thereby becoming a superior communicator.

2.5. How to Enhance Emotional Intelligence

Emotional intelligence isn't a fixed characteristic; it evolves with time and can be improved upon. To enhance emotional intelligence, earmarking time for self-reflection is essential. Other methods include practicing responsiveness, cultivating empathy by placing oneself in another's shoes, understanding personal triggers that lead to impaired judgement and inappropriate responses.

With the right amount of practice and introspection, we can train our mind to better understand our emotions and those of others, significantly improving our ability to communicate effectively.

In summary, emotional intelligence forms the cornerstone of successful communication. By understanding and managing our emotions, we can properly convey and interpret information, promoting clarity and reducing misunderstandings. Consequently, we are better equipped to form stronger bonds and navigate relational complexities, fostering healthier interactions and fruitful dialogues.

Chapter 3. Why Emotion Matters: The Science of Feelings in Communication

We often view emotions as superfluous elements when it comes to logical discourse or decision-making. Rational thought seems to be the reigning champion, dismissing feelings as a hindrance rather than an ally. But this view undersells the true power and potential of emotional intelligence. Emotions, in fact, deeply influence our capacity to communicate and connect with others. To fully grasp how and why, we delve into the fascinating science behind emotions in communication.

3.1. Emotions as Vital Messaging Tools

First and foremost, we must recognize that emotions are not an arbitrary phenomenon. They have a biological basis and a purpose. Our brains coordinate with our bodies to discern immediate reactions to the events around us, leading to what we perceive as emotions. Emotions act as shortcut indicators, telling us if a situation or interaction is potentially harmful, pleasurable, or indifferent.

The feelings you experience during a conversation are not isolated aspects of your awareness; they are biologically ingrained messenger systems that create a background context for your communication. Your emotional state significantly affects your perspective, thoughts, attitudes, and behaviors during the conversation. Incorporating emotional intelligence into our communication means acknowledging and harnessing these emotional messages rather than disregarding them.

"

3.2. The Cognitive Impact of Emotion

Our emotions also have a profound influence on the cognitive processes involved in communication. It's worth considering some key ways in which emotions impact our cognition.

Influence on Memory: Emotionally charged events are more likely to be remembered than neutral ones. This is because emotions intensify the encoding and storage of information in our brains. If you associate a specific conversation with strong emotions, you are more likely to remember the details of that conversation.

Influence on Attention: Emotions dictate where we direct our attention. Distinct emotional states lead us to focus on different aspects of a situation. If you are anxious, you may concentrate more on potential threats; if you're excited, you may focus more on the opportunities.

Influence on Decision Making: Finally, our emotions shape our decisions, even when we think we're being wholly logical. They guide us towards choices that align with our instinctive emotional reactions, fostering a harmonious connection between our subjective experiences and objective actions.

Thus, understanding and managing our emotional experiences as we communicate is not just about being 'touchy-feely' – it's about being effective.

3.3. Emotional Contagion in Communication

Now, consider this: emotions aren't just internal experiences. They are also vastly influential communicative tools.

Emotional contagion refers to the phenomenon where one person's emotions and related behaviors directly trigger similar emotions and behaviors in other people. This is not limited to face-to-face interaction; emotional contagion occurs even in digital communications.

Therefore, when we manage our own emotions effectively, we also manage the emotions we evoke in others. The mood you present in a conversation can set the tone for the entire interaction. If we approach others with positivity and empathy, those positive feelings can permeate the interaction, fostering effective and enjoyable communication.

3.4. The Crucial Role of Empathy

Empathy, a core component of emotional intelligence, is critical for effective communication. Empathy allows us to understand and share the feelings of others. It helps us respond appropriately, build rapport, and make others feel heard and understood. When we exercise empathy, we allow for a more meaningful exchange of information, ideas and emotions.

However, empathy isn't a switch that you can simply flip on when required. Like any other skill, it needs to be cultivated. Cultivating empathy involves active listening, managing your emotions, understanding non-verbal cues, and most importantly, genuine concern for the well-being of others.

3.5. In Conclusion

Emotions are more than just ephemeral experiences; they are intricately tied to our biology and cognitive processes. Grasping the science behind feelings in communication will not only make us more effective communicators but also enable us to understand others better. By harnessing our emotional intelligence, we can turn every conversation into a potential bridge of understanding and connection.

Effective communication is not solely about crafting the perfect argument or choosing the right words. At its heart, it is about understanding the emotional framework within which those words are spoken and received. As we continue on our journey through this report, we will delve further into how exactly we can harness the power of emotional intelligence to transform the way we communicate.

Chapter 4. Decoding Emotional Cues: Empathy in Effective Communication

Just as we are immersed in an invisible sea of air, we are also enveloped in an invisible sea of emotions. It sparkles in our eyes and is etched in our faces, leaking into our gestures, postures, and voice. These subtle emotional cues require careful deciphering, a process where empathy plays a key role. Empathy weaves emotional intelligence and communication together, fostering understanding and establishing genuine connection.

4.1. The Intricacies of Emotional Cues

Emotions are a non-verbal form of communication that we constantly emit. Like a river's undercurrent, they steer our interactions with others. The voice's tone, the eyes' gaze, the body's posture, and facial expressions are all emotional cues that influence communication beyond what words can express.

Are we encoding and decoding these non-verbal cues effectively, though? Let's reflect on an everyday scenario - a colleague quietly enters a meeting late, with shoulders slouched and eyes avoiding contact. Beyond the tardiness, you notice something off. You intuitively pick up their low spirits, which remains unsaid. Your decoding of the emotional cues prompts an empathetic response, changing how the meeting progresses or your personal approach to the colleague.

Understanding these emotional cues is crucial for effective communication, transforming it from a mere transfer of information into an enriching interaction that nurtures connection and mutual understanding.

4.2. The Bridge of Empathy

Empathy, the ability to understand and share the feelings of another, is one of the pillars of emotional intelligence. It invites us to step into another person's shoes, fostering a shared emotional experience. Yet, empathy isn't about losing ourselves in another's emotions; it's about recognizing, understanding, and connecting with their emotional state while maintaining a certain level of detachment.

The bridge of empathy connects the islands of our individual experiences and perspectives, fostering an understanding that words sometimes fail to convey. Consider a classic example. Two friends meet at a café. One of them is going through a tough breakup, voice trembling with pain as he narrates his story. The other sits in silence, feeling the friend's anguish as though it were his own. The empathetic silence resonates more powerfully than any advice or reassuring platitudes.

4.3. Empathy in Active Listening

The process of active listening heightens empathy in communication. While we naturally assume that communication is heavily biased towards speaking, in reality, effective communication often involves more listening than talking. Active listening hinges on being fully present in the conversation, focusing on the speaker, reflecting what they've said, and resisting the temptation to formulate responses while they are still talking.

Active listening, accentuated with empathy, takes us beyond hearing the spoken words to understanding the emotions they carry. This shift deepens communication, fostering a shared understanding and enhancing our response's effectiveness.

4.4. Empathy in Non-Verbal Communication

While verbal cues are vital, non-verbal cues provide valuable emotional context to our communication networks. Body language, facial expressions, eye contact, and tone of voice convey emotions more honestly than words can often do. An empathetic communicator learns to decode these non-verbal cues, gaining a richer understanding of the emotional landscape being navigated.

Consider a manager conveying a tough decision to her team. She softens her tone, maintains steady eye contact, and uses open body language. These non-verbal cues reinforce her empathetic approach, assuring the team that the decision was tough on her too. It conveys the unsaid yet crucial message: she understands their emotions and is with them through the challenge.

4.5. Empathy as A Responsive Mechanism

Empathy also serves as a feedback mechanism, shaping our responses in communication. An empathetic response acknowledges the other person's emotional state and communicates understanding. This has a validating effect, often helping the other person to manage their emotions better.

Imagine a heated argument where both participants are primarily focused on making their point. If one of them pauses, acknowledges the other's frustration, and empathetically responds, it could likely deescalate the situation. The emotionally intelligent communicator knows that responding with empathy isn't about agreeing with the other person's perspective but validating their emotions.

4.6. Empathy and Emotional Regulation

Empathy goes hand in hand with emotional regulation - another key element of emotional intelligence. Emotion regulation is about recognizing our emotions and managing them to foster effective communication. It's crucial to respond rather than react, especially in emotionally charged situations. Emotional regulation helps cultivate a more empathetic response, recognizing the emotions at play, both ours and others, and choosing our steps wisely to facilitate better communication.

Clearly, empathy transcends being just an attribute to a crucial skill in the realm of effective communication. As we become more attuned to the emotional cues around us and respond empathetically, our conversations become more connected, rich and meaningful. Communication, thus, becomes not just a transmission of information, but a tool to build connections and strengthen relations with others. Embrace empathy and revolutionize your communication with the power of emotional intelligence.

Chapter 5. The Power of Patience: Emotional Control in Dialogue

Patience, as we've often heard, is a virtue. It's an essential component in the process of effective communication and emotional control - an encapsulating door to dialogue that promotes understanding and harmony. Let's delve into how patience and emotional restraint influence conversations, based on the expert insights, research findings, and practical examples.

5.1. Why Patience Matters in Dialogue

A dialogue is more than an exchange of words; it's an intertwined dance of thoughts, emotions, and intentions. Patience is the rhythm that guides this dance, allowing it to flow seamlessly.

Consider a scenario where one participant hurriedly interjects, seeking to hurriedly impose their point of view. This rush not only impedes understanding but can also create an environment of hostility. On the contrary, a patient listener, who takes the time to understand the sentiments behind the words before responding, contributes to a more positive and fruitful exchange.

There's a term in psychology - "affect labeling" - which describes how recognizing and naming our emotions helps in managing them better. Patience is quintessential in this process as it allows us time to pause, reflect, and label our emotions accurately.

Furthermore, patience in dialogue contributes to emotional intelligence. It helps us retain control over our responses, ensuring they are reasoned rather than impulsive. That said, the question then arises - how do we actualize patience in our dialogues?

5.2. Cultivating Patience: Strategies to Foster Equilibrium in Conversations

Mastering patience is a journey, often marked by self-exploration, practice, and resilience. Here are some key strategies to foster patience within conversations:

1. **Self-Reflection**: Before entering a dialogue, take a moment to breath and assess your emotions. Underline your thought process, and mentally set a patient tone for the upcoming communication.

2. **Active Listening**: This means wholly concentrating on the speaker, understanding their message, and responding thoughtfully. Active listening is a form of respect and promotes a patient, balanced dialogue.

3. **Mindfulness**: It refers to fully engaging in the present, calmly accepting feelings and thoughts. Incorporating mindfulness in conversations sparks patience by encouraging thoughtful responses over reactive replies.

4. **Stress management**: Stress often prompts us to respond hastily in dialogues. Techniques like yoga, meditation, deep breathing, or even simple practices like taking a walk or listening to calming music can help manage stress levels, promoting emotional control in conversations.

5.3. The Role of Emotional Control

While patience sets the pace, emotional control determines the direction of a conversation. Emotions can be subtle, swift, and often overwhelming. Yet, they are crucial to understanding human communication since they influence how we interpret information and how we react.

Emotional control is essentially the ability to manage and direct our emotions constructively. It's the bridge between experiencing an emotion and articulating a response.

Consider heated arguments, for instance. Without emotional control, these arguments quickly spiral, causing both parties to dig in their heels. However, with emotional control, we can break this cycle, redirecting the conversation towards resolution.

Emotional control in dialogue prioritizes understanding over winning, harmony over conflict. But how do we achieve this control?

5.4. Achieving Emotional Control: Tips for More Balanced Dialogues

Achieving emotional control in dialogues doesn't mean suppressing emotions. Instead, it involves understanding them, acknowledging their existence and guiding their expression in a beneficial manner. Here are some suggestions:

1. **Emotional Awareness**: Recognizing your emotional state is the first step. Note any emotional shifts during a conversation, identify these emotions, and try to discern their triggers.

2. **Self-Regulation**: Once you're aware of your emotions and their triggers, you can manage them more effectively. This involves restraint and careful consideration of the potential impacts of your emotional reactions. Meditation can facilitate self-regulation by helping you develop a calm, detached perspective towards these emotions.

3. **Constructive Expression**: Not all emotions are negative. Positively channeling even 'negative' emotions can stimulate constructive discussions. For instance, if a conversation makes you feel frustrated, try expressing this in a non-confrontational manner. You might say, "I'm feeling somewhat frustrated because I feel like I'm not being understood. Can I explain my point again?"

Discovering the balance between emotional expression and emotional control is undoubtedly challenging. However, enduring this challenge can significantly enhance your communication skills, driving more meaningful, influential dialogues.

In conclusion, both patience and emotional control are significant influencers of successful dialogues. They enable us to tune into our emotional intelligence, fostering conversations that are not centered on conflicts or contention, but on understanding, collaboration, and growth.

Chapter 6. Using Positivity: The Connection Between Happiness and Communication

One cannot stress enough the profound influence happiness has on our communication skills. The two are not just subtly intertwined but intensely interconnected. This relationship, in all its depth and variations, can be explored through the lens of optimism, mindset, relationships, and the myriad forms of communication we encounter daily.

6.1. The Optimistic Lens

Psychology tells us that positivity or happiness influences not only how we perceive the world but also how the world perceives us. This lends itself to the concept of emotional contagion, a psychological phenomenon where we tend to "catch" emotions from those around us. Walking into a room with a positive attitude instantly changes the air, making conversations more open and effective.

The optimism bias further elucidates the impact of positivity on our communication. This cognitive bias compels humans to believe that they are more likely to experience positive events and less likely to experience negative ones. Optimists are seen as better communicators. They effectively voice their thoughts and are good at listening, resulting in positive social encounters and strong interpersonal relationships.

6.2. The Component of Mindset

Positivity is more than a fleeting emotion - it is a mindset. A positive mindset springs from self-esteem, resilience, and a constructive perspective towards failure. Individuals with a positive disposition view adversities as opportunities for growth, thereby influencing not just their communication but also their overall life views.

Carol Dweck's work on 'Fixed versus Growth Mindset' investigates this idea further. Those with a growth mindset, characterized by being open to new experiences and showcasing resilience, are more likely to be effective communicators. Their proclivity for sincere conversation and constructive feedback promotes a conducive communication environment.

6.3. Happiness and Relationships

A Harvard Study tracking the lives of 724 men over 75 years pinpointed good relationships as the key to happiness. But it's a two-way street – happiness fuels quality relationships and quality relationships stir happiness. And at the heart of quality relationships lies effective communication.

This translates to all kinds of relationships, personal and professional. Happiness can breed trust, empathy, and mutual respect, all vital components for meaningful communication. Happy individuals are more likely to express these traits in their interactions, enriching their relationships and consequently nourishing their happiness.

6.4. Areas of Application

So far, we have explored how happiness spills over into effective communication. This section will delve into the myriad ways this connection plays out across varied forms of communication.

6.4.1. Written communication:

Whether it's an email, a text message, a report, or even a social media post, written communication is infused with our emotional state. Happy individuals tend to use more positive language, leading to clearer, more engaging, and highly effective written communication.

6.4.2. Verbal communication:

Tone, pitch, volume, and speed of speech – all vital parts of verbal communication – are impacted by our emotional state. Happiness usually comes with a steady, warm, and assured vocal tone that often translates into effective and persuasive verbal communication.

6.4.3. Non-verbal communication:

Our emotions strongly influence our body language. Open gestures, expressiveness, and a relaxed demeanor are associated with happiness and communicated effectively to the observer, often resulting in enriched conversations.

6.5. Reflections and Implementations

Awareness of the connection between happiness and communication is an enlightening realization but using it to enhance one's communication requires deliberate effort. Here are a few strategies:

6.5.1. Cultivate Positivity:

Positive emotions can be fostered through gratitude, mindfulness, and affirmations. Engage in activities you love, surround yourself with encouraging people, and take care of your physical health.

6.5.2. Embrace a growth mindset:

Dedicate time for learning and self-reflection. Accept failure as a stepping stone towards growth and appreciate feedback.

6.5.3. Invest in relationships:

Positive interactions form the basis of all successful relationships. Honest communication, displaying empathy, and showing respect are assured ways to enrich connections.

6.5.4. Master communication platforms:

Identify your areas of strength and opportunities for growth across different forms of communication. Practice positivity, be it in a written report, a presentation, or casual conversation.

It's essential to remember that incorporating positivity into communication, just like any skill, requires time, patience, and persistence. The journey may be challenging at times, but the resultant effective communication makes it all worthwhile.

To conclude, the magnanimity of happiness transcends beyond its pleasing facet. It underpins successful communication, making conversations meaningful, relationships rewarding, and life fulfilling. That is the power of positivity – it makes us happy and, in turn, makes us better communicators. So get started on this journey of positive communication right away; it's never too late to tap into the endless possibilities of effective conversation.

Chapter 7. Breaking Down Barriers: Overcoming Emotional Obstacles in Communication

There are several emotional barriers that can affect our communication, both consciously and subconsciously. Understanding these obstacles and learning to confront them can drastically enhance the quality of our conversations with others.

7.1. Recognizing Emotional Barriers

Before we can begin to dismantle emotional barriers and hone our communication skills, we must first learn to recognize them. These barriers can present themselves in myriad ways, such as anger, fear, anxiety, apathy, and more. For instance, the fear of judgment can cause us to reserve our thoughts, whereas anger can prevent us from listening effectively to others.

Understanding the origin of these barriers is fundamental to overcoming them. Emotional triggers often have roots in past experiences and traumas. Becoming aware of these triggers and understanding the way they affect our communication is the first step to overcoming them. Mindfulness exercises, self-reflection, and even professional help can aid in this process.

7.2. Emotions and Their Impact on Communication

Emotions profoundly impact the way we communicate. They

influence the words we use, our body language, and even the tone of our voice. When our emotions run high, they can easily cloud our judgment and decrease our ability to communicate effectively.

For instance, fear and anxiety can cause us to overthink and misinterpret signals from others. Anger can lead to aggression, hindering open communication. And apathy, if not addressed correctly, can lead to disengagement or indifference.

To overcome these barriers, we first need to learn the art of emotional regulation. This involves understanding and managing our emotions in a way that allows them to aid, rather than hinder, our communication.

7.3. Emotional Regulation and Effective Communication

Emotion regulation is the process of identifying, understanding, and controlling our emotions. By practicing emotional regulation, we can develop emotional intelligence, which further enables us to communicate our feelings effectively and empathize with others' emotions.

Self-awareness is crucial in emotional regulation. We need to regularly check in with ourselves and how we're feeling. Using techniques like mindfulness, journaling or reflective practice can help build this self-awareness.

Next, we need to develop strategies for managing strong emotions. Breathing exercises, meditation, and even simply taking a pause before responding can help us regulate our emotions during communication.

Emotional regulation also requires resilience. It's all about understanding that it's okay to feel certain emotions and knowing that they will pass. By learning to ride the emotional waves instead of suppressing them, we become adept at self-regulation.

7.4. Empathy and its Role in Overcoming Barriers

Empathy plays a crucial role in overcoming emotional barriers in communication. A key component of emotional intelligence, empathy is the ability to understand and share the feelings of others.

In communication, empathy allows us to better understand where the other person is coming from, which increases the chance of successful communication. By listening attentively, we can pick up on the emotions behind their words, allowing us to respond in a thoughtful and understanding manner.

Developing empathy involves learning to step out of our perspective and into another's shoes. It means suspending our judgments and seeking to comprehend the other person's point of view. This practice doesn't come naturally to everyone, but consistent practice helps to enhance our empathic abilities.

Empathy also fosters emotional availability, which means being open about our feelings and inviting others to do the same. When emotions are expressed honestly and openly, it promotes a communication environment that is free of misunderstandings and assumptions.

7.5. Techniques & Tools for Enhancing Emotional Intelligence

To effectively navigate the realm of emotions in communication, we need to arm ourselves with the right techniques and tools. These might include practices like mindfulness, cognitive restructuring, and assertive communication.

Mindfulness involves staying present and focused during our interactions. It encourages us to approach the conversation with curiosity and open-mindedness rather than judgment or defensiveness.

Cognitive restructuring entails changing the negative thinking patterns that cloud our communication. For instance, instead of assuming the worst, we can train ourselves to see the situation from different angles and assess it more objectively.

Assertive communication means expressing our thoughts and feelings openly, honestly, and respectfully, while also considering and accepting the feelings and opinions of others.

By learning and practicing these techniques regularly, we can significantly enhance our emotional intelligence, thereby breaking down the emotional barriers that stand in the way of effective communication.

In conclusion, overcoming emotional barriers in communication is a journey of self-awareness, emotional regulation, empathy, and resilience. Though it requires consistent effort and practice, the reward of clearer, more effective communication is immeasurable.

Chapter 8. Combatting Misunderstandings: Emotional Clarity in Conversations

Miscommunication and misunderstandings can often be the root of conflicts in our personal and professional lives. But what if we told you that there's a tool available, one that could help you sort through the traps of miscommunication, and pave the way for clear, effective, and mutual understanding? This tool is not elusive or exclusive; it's nicely nested within all of us: Emotional Intelligence (EI).

The art of understanding, utilizing, and responding to emotions effectively, EI is about being "emotionally smart". It's a skill that empowers us to recognize both our emotions and those of others, thus fostering understanding, reducing conflicts, and improving relationships. This part of our report will dive deep into understanding how EI can help us combat misunderstandings and improve clarity in our conversations.

8.1. Understand Your Emotions

One fundamental aspect of EI is self-awareness, the ability to recognise and understand our own emotions. This is vital in communication because our emotions deeply influence how we interpret information and respond to it. If we're unaware of our emotions, they can stealthily control our communication style, leading to possible friction and misunderstandings.

Emotion recognition is a stepping stone to emotional understanding. This is not just about identifying when we feel sad, angry, or happy, but also about understanding 'why'. Decoding the 'why' can help unpick the essence of your feelings, helping to change the course of conversations from conflict to resolution.

But how can we develop this understanding? Reflective practices like journaling, mindfulness and meditation can be useful. These exercises foster an inward focus, helping us zero in on our emotional triggers and responses.

8.2. Emotional Control

Heightened emotions can cloud judgment, escalate conflicts, and skew conversations. Thus, it's important not just to recognize our emotions but to manage them effectively. Emotional control refers to our ability to stay composed and keep our emotions in check, especially in high-pressure situations or during difficult conversations.

Emotional control doesn't mean suppressing emotions. After all, emotions are natural, and each one has a role to play. They're valuable indicators of our reactions to situations or people. Instead, emotional control is about understanding our emotional responses and expressing them appropriately.

Emotional control requires consistent effort. Techniques like deep-breathing, stepping back, taking time to respond, or even deciding to revisit a conversation when you're calmer can be beneficial.

8.3. Recognizing Emotions in Others

EI isn't just about understanding our own emotions; it's also about attuning to others' emotions. This is called empathy, a crucial tool in combating misunderstandings.

When we empathize, we see through the other person's perspective, understanding their feelings and reactions. This can provide context and depth to our conversations, as we interpret their words and actions not merely from our viewpoint but theirs as well. Furthermore, demonstrating understanding of others' emotions can make them feel validated and heard, promoting positive, effective communication.

Active listening is key to developing empathy. It requires fully focusing, understanding, responding, and then remembering what is being said in a conversation. It also involves recognizing and understanding non-verbal cues, which often communicate more than words.

8.4. Emotional Expression

Understanding our own and others' emotions won't make much of a difference unless we express this understanding. Emotional expression, the final aspect of EI, is the act of communicating our feelings and needs openly and effectively.

An accusation or harsh words can push the conversation towards an argument, while expressing the same feeling differently can lead to a problem-solving discussion. The difference lies in how we express our emotions. Effective emotional expression ensures we're clear, avoid blame, remain respectful, and assert our needs, thereby reducing misunderstandings.

One key technique here is the use of 'I' statements, for example, saying "I felt disappointed when the deadline was missed," instead of "You missed the deadline and ruined everything." This shifts the focus from blaming others to expressing how their actions impacted us.

Clarity in conversations is not just about the right choice of words. It's also about encoding messages with the right emotional tone. Equipped with self-awareness, emotional control, empathy, and effective emotional expression, we can significantly reduce miscommunication and the misunderstandings that usually follow.

Our conversations will not purely be exchanges of words but engaging interactions laden with empathy, mutual respect, and understanding. All of this is made possible by the power of Emotional Intelligence. Call it emotional clarity or emotional literacy, EI equips us with the tools to transform our conversations and connections, bringing us all closer to a world of effective, insightful communication. Through this understanding of emotions, we don't just become better communicators. We become better listeners, partners, co-workers, and ultimately, better human beings.

Our understanding of Emotional Intelligence and its profound impacts on conversations doesn't have to stop here. Dive deeper into the fascinating world of EI with our report, delving into the numerous other ways it can transform conversations, and indeed, lives. Harness the power of your emotions; it's time to communicate clearly, honestly, and effectively.

Chapter 9. Motivating Dialogue: Using Emotional Intelligence to Inspire Discussion

Every discourse holds the potential to inspire, motivate, and transform. How we steer these conversations, especially those challenging ones, determines their impact on both us and our dialogical counterparts. This exploration begins by understanding and exploiting the cardinal tool in our navigational repertoire: Emotional Intelligence (EI).

9.1. Embracing Emotional Intelligence

Emotional intelligence is more than identifying our feelings. It's a comprehensive understanding of our emotional landscape, paired with the ability to harness these feelings to manage behavior, navigate social complexities, and make personal decisions that lead to positive outcomes. It encompasses four primary skills: self-awareness, self-management, social awareness, and relationship management.

With the right dose of emotional intelligence, one can tweak their communication to motivate dialogues and inspire discussions. But before we dig deeper into these nuances, let's acquaint ourselves with the very constructs of EI.

9.2. Core Constructs of Emotional Intelligence

9.2.1. Self-Awareness

The journey of emotional intelligence begins within ourselves. Self-awareness involves recognizing our emotions as they occur and understanding the impact they can have on our thoughts and actions. It's about connecting the dots between our feelings, beliefs, and behaviors and recognizing the patterns that emerge.

9.2.2. Self-Management

Once we're mindful of our emotions, the next step is managing them. Self-management revolves around controlling and redirecting disruptive feelings and impulses and adjusting to changing circumstances. It's not about suppressing feelings, but about appropriate expression at the right time.

9.2.3. Social Awareness

Stepping out of ourselves, we venture into the realm of social awareness: the ability to understand the emotions, needs, and concerns of others. It involves empathy and the knack to pick up emotional cues, often exhibited in verbal and non-verbal communications.

9.2.4. Relationship Management

The climax of this EI journey is relationship management. This skill is about clear communication, conflict management, inspiration delivery, and fostering instrumental connections. It's about using our awareness of our and others' emotions to manage interactions successfully.

9.3. EI and Motivating Dialogue

With a rooted understanding of emotional intelligence's core constructs, we can now delve into how to apply this framework to inspire dialogues that gratify, enlighten, and spur change.

9.3.1. Emotionally Intelligent Conversations

Every conversation is an emotional transaction. Whether it's a simple exchange with a colleague or a deep discussion with your partner, our feelings significantly flavor these dialogues. Here's how you can mesh the four domains of EI into your communication:

1. **Self-Awareness**: Observe your thoughts and feelings during the conversation. Monitor your emotional responses and identify any triggers. This self-awareness helps to steer the dialogue effectively.

2. **Self-Management**: Utilize your emotional insights to calibrate your responses. Manage any undesirable emotions that may hinder the conversation and act to de-escalate tensions.

3. **Social Awareness**: Pay ardent attention to the other person's verbal and non-verbal cues. Understand their state of mind and emotional place to tailor the dialogue and foster deeper understanding.

4. **Relationship Management**: Through active empathetic listening and emotionally charged feedback, keep their interests in mind while fostering collaboration or resolving any disagreements.

9.3.2. Inspiring Others through EI

Inspiring others through emotional intelligence is about generating a sense of motivation and creating an atmosphere that encourages open dialogues. Here are some strategies:

1. **Empathetic Listening**: Demonstrate empathy. It encourages others to open up and share their thoughts and feelings. This level of deep understanding enables inspiring dialogues.

2. **Emotionally Charged Feedback**: Give constructive, emotionally intelligent feedback. It should be truthful, clear, non-judgmental, and aimed at encouraging growth and learning.

3. **Express Authenticity**: Authenticity builds trust and rapport. Show your genuine intention in understanding and engaging with others.

4. **Encourage Emotional Expression**: Create an environment where emotional expression is welcomed and respected. This democratizes the power of emotions in the conversation.

Emotional intelligence, when integrated into our dialogues, can empower us to touch depths that might have been unthinkable otherwise. Tread the path of self-awareness, self-management, social awareness, and relationship management to motivate discussions like never before, and savor the profound transformations such dialogues can bring about. Let emotional intelligence be the navigator that steers your conversation ship towards a horizon marked with understanding, connection, and mutual growth.

Chapter 10. Navigating Difficult Conversations: The Balance of Emotional Sensitivity

In this complex world where one's ability to articulate thoughts critically impacts their relations, success, and quality of life, navigating difficult conversations remains a key skill. Emotional sensitivity is an integral element that, when wielded appropriately, can make a significant difference.

10.1. The Importance of Emotional Sensitivity

Emotional sensitivity, which is a crucial aspect of emotional intelligence, stands at the forefront of these efforts. It is defined as the capacity to perceive, process, and react to emotional stimuli in oneself and others. Many people avoid difficult conversations because they're uncomfortable experiencing or causing negative emotions. Yet, skillfully navigating such dialogues relies on our ability to understand and manage emotions effectively.

While emotional sensitivity has sometimes been stigmatized as excessive or unnecessary, the latest in psychological research extols its profound strengths. It enhances our capacity for empathy, understanding, and connection. It allows us to engage with difficult conversations with greater nuance, creating opportunities for resolution where others may see only conflict.

10.2. The Balance Between Logic and Emotion

The balancing act between logic and emotion is the common tightrope walked in every difficult conversation. Too much emotion can cloud judgment, inhibit problem-solving abilities, and escalate the situation. On the other hand, being overly logical can erode inter-human connections, give offense, and make solutions seem cold and uncaring.

This balance is delicate. It requires us to embrace the usefulness of emotions, such as the vital information they provide about our internal state and values, without letting them overrule our rational thought. In the other direction, we must use logic to structure our arguments without neglecting the emotional context through which our words will be received.

10.3. Developing Emotional Awareness

High emotional awareness is the foundation of emotional sensitivity. Awareness is observing and reflecting on our internal emotional landscape and understanding how it interacts with our thoughts and actions.

For example, envision yourself in a heated conversation. You might feel anger and defensiveness. Emotional awareness would allow you to recognize these rising emotions, understand that they stem from feeling attacked, and realize that retaliating could escalate the conversation without solving the issue.

Developing emotional awareness involves practices such as mindfulness meditation, journaling about emotional experiences, and simply checking in with yourself throughout the day.

10.4. Recognizing and Navigating Emotional Triggers

Everyone has emotional triggers—specific instances, words, or actions—that evoke a strong emotional reaction. These triggers often correlate with unresolved issues or conflict areas in one's life. Being taken by surprise by these triggers during a tough conversation can lead to unhelpful emotional responses.

Recognizing our triggers requires introspection and honesty. Once identified, we can prepare ourselves for potential triggering during difficult conversations and create strategies to navigate the resulting emotional turbulence. This could involve taking deep breaths to calm down, asking for a short break, or practicing positive reaffirmations.

10.5. Showing Empathy and Active Listening

A critical aspect of emotional sensitivity is the capacity for empathy—that is, understanding and sharing the feelings of others. This trait allows us to make personal connections and build trust, creating an environment where a productive dialogue can take place.

Active listening is an effective method of demonstrating empathy. It involves paying full attention to the speaker, avoiding any distractions, and providing feedback that shows you've accurately received their message. This form of listening fosters connection and trust, which are essential for successful difficult conversations.

10.6. Reframing Negativity and Conflict

Negativity and conflict are inevitable parts of difficult conversations. However, how we interpret such challenging situations greatly affects their outcomes.

Reframing is a common psychological tool used to alter our conception of a negative event. This doesn't mean denying reality or putting a false positive spin on the situation. Instead, it's a cognitive shift towards a more objective or constructive perspective. If mastered, reframing can transform the way we approach conflict and negativity.

In summary, effective and sensitive navigation of the treacherous terrains of difficult conversations requires emotional sensitivity, which can be nurtured through emotional awareness, identifying emotional triggers, empathy, active listening, and reframing negativity. Recognizing and respecting the delicate balance between logic and emotions can help convert difficult conversations into opportunities for growth and connection. This acumen forms an integral part of the holistic development of one's emotional intelligence, thereby fostering successful communication in all walks of life.

Chapter 11. The Future Forecast: Next Steps in Emotional Intelligence and Communication

In recent times, scholars and industry leaders have been shining a spotlight on the art of emotional intelligence – the ability to identify, understand, and manage our emotions and those of others. We've already uncovered how this precious skill leads to effective communication. But the journey doesn't end here.

It's not merely about having emotional intelligence; rather, it's about how we apply this intelligence to navigate the complex channels of human communication. As we step into tomorrow, this area necessitates further exploration and development.

11.1. Exploring the Emotional Landscape

A fundamental understanding of emotions rests at the core of emotional intelligence. Emotions are not just internal experiences, but are communicative signals that influence the feelings and actions of those around us. Recent research has shown how human emotion, far from being entirely personal, has broader social implications. Harnessing the communicative potential of emotions will be a cornerstone in refining our utilization of emotional intelligence.

Tomorrow's leaders must be adept at identifying and understanding both their emotions and those of others. Subtleties in emotional displays can reveal a great deal about colleagues or clients. Moreover, empathizing with these emotions can foster productive and meaningful relationships. What might seem an incidental tear or a twinkling smirk can be a window into another person's inner world.

Future research should focus on developing tools and techniques that enhance our emotional awareness. Moreover, emotional education must be widespread, moving beyond the confines of academia and boardrooms to reach every individual, strengthening communal ties and fostering healthy communication.

11.2. Application in the Digital Sphere

In an increasingly digital world, effective communication goes beyond face-to-face interaction. The internet and social media have transformed how we express and interpret emotions, and our emotional intelligence must evolve with it.

Social media platforms have a wide range of emoticons, GIFs, and other expressive assets to help communicate our emotions when words alone seem insufficient. These emotional cues, though synthetic, help create a shared emotional reality in digital spaces.

For instance, research indicates that positive posts generate more positive posts in response, creating an emotional ripple effect. In contrast, negative posts generate more negativity. The way we control our online emotional expression can influence the online emotional climate.

The future of emotional intelligence will involve focusing on how we can leverage digital communication tools to promote a more positive and empathic online environment. Additionally, businesses must consider how emotional intelligence can be utilized in digital customer interactions.

11.3. Automating Emotional Intelligence

Emotional artificial intelligence, or Emotion AI, is an emerging field, looking to bridge cognitive computing with human emotions. It aims to develop machines that understand and respond to human emotions, simultaneously advancing and challenging our understanding of emotional intelligence.

We've already seen the development of automated systems that recognize basic human emotions through facial and vocal cues. Recently, software algorithms have been used to analyze emotions via text-based communication.

In the near future, we can expect further evolution of Emotion AI. It could feasibly assist in virtual therapy sessions, customer service roles, and in analyzing public sentiment around products or social issues. As we develop these technologies, we must also contemplate the implications and ethical considerations of non-human entities processing human emotions.

11.4. Personal Growth and Development

The future of emotional intelligence and communication rests on personal development. It's a lifelong journey, not a destination one can reach. A commitment to ongoing learning, emotional growth, and adapting to new emotional landscapes is crucial.

To this end, mindfulness exercises can play a significant role. Mindfulness helps us anchor ourselves in the present, pay deliberate attention to our feelings, and respond to them constructively. There are apps, online courses, and self-help books dedicated to fostering mindfulness and emotional self-awareness.

As we move forward, democratizing accessibility to such resources will be vital. Emotional intelligence should be considered a universal right, available to all in order to promote healthier mental states, stronger relationships, and effective communication.

In conclusion, the future of emotional intelligence and communication is bright and deeply interconnected. As we work to expand our understanding, we should keep in mind the intimate relationship between our inner emotional landscapes, digital emotional expressions, the rise of Emotion AI, and our commitment to personal growth and mindful progress.

www.ingramcontent.com/pod-product-compliance
Lightning Source LLC
Chambersburg PA
CBHW071014260726
48661CB00007B/2962